Songs of Youth

Ayanna Newman

Grosvenor House
Publishing Limited

This book is published by
Grosvenor House Publishing Ltd
Link House
140 The Broadway, Tolworth, Surrey, KT6 7HT.
www.grosvenorhousepublishing.co.uk

A CIP record for this book
is available from the British Library

ISBN 978-1-80381-441-4

Dedicated

To those grassroots dwellers who lent a sentence
or a word to my work.

Give thanks

Contents

Rain

It's Saturday
and
it's raining
sleet
kind of
icy
rain.

Rain being
water
dropping from
the sky.
You know
that interaction
of meteorological elements
in the
atmosphere.

Now
snow is almost
the same thing
only
snowflakes quite like
soap flakes
depending on how they
fall
may take
a long time to
dissipate.

contd/over

Slipping
sliding
cutting
car wheels rutting
but
we soon
learn
to cope.

A Poem

This
poem
finished
the
second
it begun
this piece of prose
speaks
silently
of
guns.

Futility (1984)

One stone
in the hand
of Azanian men
left
19 Africans dead
one stone
not thrown
just poised
I said
and
19 Africans
were filled with lead.

They claim
bombs
were thrown instead
to justify
a
racist
murderous
trend
that's left countless
Africans
stone cold dead.

Peace prizes
given like bread
to eliminate the
eye for eye

contd/over

trend.
Bible and religion
in our heads
instead of
guns
in our hands
I said.

While
everyday
more of our people
lay
dead
for
peacefully mourning
burying
their dead.

While
more and more
Africans
are
shot
in the head
jus take up the gun
I said
to obliterate
the
racist
murderous
trend
to put up
'gainst
Apartheid's
head.

Perched

I wish I was
a man
some times.

Perched
tall
in a blues
with my
flannel
to my face.

Head buoyant
to the
riddim
of the
bass.

I wish
I was
a man
some times.

Shotgun (Colin Roach)

Shotgun holes
were blasted
through
his head.

A young man
lies dead
slumped
at the door
of a
Police station
dead.

Shot
fighting
to get in.
Shot
pleading
let me in,
escaping.

Shot
in a
suicidal
jest.
Shotgun barrel
blasts
a black youth
to his
death.

Travelling

I sat there
quietly
on this Tube
when a drunken man
flew in
like a gale force
abusing
cursing
you
the skies
the heavens
then you.

He sat down
mused
on who
to interfere with.
Chose me
rather than
the woman
opposite
embarrassed.

Wishing
he would
go away.
But I saw
he had something
to say

contd/over

as he leered
at me
"You don't want to speak to me 'cos you're black".
And
I wondered
who raised the issue
anyway
is this man
really referring to me
he must be.
So, like I didn't hear
I turned my head
"I'm sorry. What was that you said"
and the question
raised order
in his
consciousness
that he had
offended me
for no reason
I had done him
no harm.
So he staggered noisily
away but
to sit next to
a little black girl
on the train.
With alcohol odours

contd/over

stifling her
causing terror
to rise in her.
"I am not safe.
Let me sit
in some
other place".
And, she came
and sat next to me
in the corner
her eyes
fluttering
within the reflection
of a tube window.
The woman opposite
who had said
nothing
said
"That's his problem"
dissociating herself
while I
said
nothing
just registered
the fact
she had expected
something else from me
having just had
my being attacked.
And, with
dark calmness
I looked at her

contd/over

forced her to register
that being black
within her context
was not my yardstick.
The little girl
sitting next to me
was still afraid.
Wondering if the corners
would really
afford protection
from this sometimes
terrifying
world.
She couldn't speak
yet uttered softly
"I am afraid".
And, I saw that little girl
right there
inside of me
and I asked her
"Are you afraid?"
She nodded

I told her
not to be,
"You'll be ok you'll see"
as the Tube train
stopped
at
the Grove.
And, when we parted
something in her
smiled at me
and
I caught it.

Considerations Nuclear

Grey misty day
on
structures
children
laugh and play.
Slide off slopes
climb
thick ropes
young lives
filled with hope
on
a
grey misty day.

Grey misty day
watching
the children
laugh and play.
A
missile

could
slide off a slope
there'd be
no structures

contd/over

no thick ropes
no lives
filled with hope
on
a
grey
misty
day.

For Granma

She has hands
that neither
mould or shape.
Her fingers
long weary
from the coffee bean
like some.

She has hands
that
mould and shape
no
world.
On her finger
the bean
had lay balanced,
scored and shaped
by the old
country woman
in her dreams.

As she
moulds no shape
memories
other word songs
meander
through
scenic lanes

contd/over

some would call
no lane
but
jagged stone
on which
dare I say
only
fools pass.

She
moulds no shape
in a
cloistered world
of spices
while

spices
sing
pimento
to a forgotten
world of toil

She moulds no shape.

Mas George

The earth
feel
look
of a place.
Tree bark
grass blades
hummingbirds
ziiiiiiiiiiiiiiiig.

Fruit
as it grows
on
a tree
from a
inviting green
to a colour
briefly
to be
seen.

All we do
is think
of our stomachs.

We used to whitewash
those
pathstones
that
led up to the

contd/over

turquoise and orange house
where granma lives.
Swim in streams
shaded by tall trees.
Look to reach
the top of
needle monument
to the dead.
Is Mas George
put it there
to his wife
no ordinary grave
dug and marked.

Broken tribunes
brief tributes
born 1819
died 1901.

Reggie

We always want it
to be dark
and
quiet.

A little country window
to the glow
of the lamp.
That loud darkness
of the night
campfires
and the night.

Where a man
he walks blind
he knows
every stone
skin tight to the bone.
That loud darkness
of
the drums
camp fires
and
the
drums.

We always want it
to be
dark.

Crickets Rock

Crickets rock
like the sound
of a
hard
reggae bass.
Tweeters
disco flash lights
race.
Storm
eena
Jamaica
sky by night.

Mosquito tents
and
tourists for rent.
Sting sting sting
for the
Dollar cent.
Sting the tourist
eena

reggae scent.
Sniff ma'am
spliff
coke
nuh badda scowl
we ahnya
jus a joke.

contd/over

Come we walk
down de road
where there is no play
on J$20 a day
people jus ah pray
bare feet eena street
fi a likkle
some ting some ting
to eat
feel sweet.

Others jus shout
Hush up yu mout
kiss u teet
nuh badda bawl life sweet.

Reggae music
ah
tump
de
street.

The Green Dress

There she was
this girl
in
a
beautiful
green dress
made of
squares.

Her head
was like
there was
a golden
rope
tied in her stomach
and up through
her head.
And something
was holding on
tight
at the other end.

When she spoke
her Martinique
accent showed.
She was in London
studying batik
in that
beautiful green dress

contd/over

made of squares.
Sewn together
the pieces
sewn together
by her own
fair hand.

She said
she had a plan
she's back there now
making
dresses
from
squares.